Y0-CBB-306

FIRE, FURY, FAITH

Fire, Fury, Faith:
A Story of Success by Fire

Roderick K. Mitchell

Foreword by Jessica Cabness, Ph.D.

ENDORSEMENTS

Fire, Fury, Faith is a moving personal account of self-rescue. I am certain that the learned RECEO techniques and principles applied to Roderick Mitchell's own journey as a professional firefighter and motivational speaker will help others.

-*Lorraine Ohara*

As a Toastmasters speaker and motivator, Roderick Mitchell polished his speaking and distinguished himself as a contest winner through long hours of practice—a process that required self-confidence and persistence. In *Fire, Fury, Faith*, Mitchell shows how he learned to apply the five-step system he used to extinguish fires and save lives to solving the problems— some routine, some threatening—of his personal life. He will take you down the same path and show you how you can use the same tools to overcome problems that you face.

-*Mike Schultz, Member, Toastmasters International*

Within the following pages lie the heart and soul of Roderick Mitchell. It is not often that an author bears all in such a concise and transparent format in order to motivate the reader to take life-changing courses of action. With each personal story, Mitchell teaches the RECEO concept in a way that best accommodates swift life application. Are you ready for meaningful change? Get into this accelerated version of Roderick Mitchell's acclaimed course to create your best life and finish strong!

-Elyce Eddings, Owner/CEO, Georgetown Nanny

Fire, Fury, Faith: A Story of Success by Fire is driven by the desire to be of service, to help others while providing a map, with directions stemming from lifelong lessons— lessons with proven results. You will find a clear and vivid picture that will remove the obstacles from your journey toward your desired destination. I have witnessed Roderick Mitchell brighten the dim lights of minds by sharing what he knows to be tried and true with his audiences. Take heed, and with your new light muster up the fire, fury, and faith within to walk your path.

-James Brown

Fire, Fury, Faith: A Story of Success by Fire

Copyright © 2019 by Roderick K. Mitchell.
All rights reserved. This book may not be
reproduced in whole or in part by any means
without permission from the author.

This book is not intended to treat or diagnose any mental
health condition. All directives, interventions, and ideas
should be used by professionals within the appropriate
bounds of their education, training, and scope of practice.

Names used are the products of the author's life, and have
been changed to protect identities. Any resemblance to
actual persons, living or dead, is purely coincidental.

 Published by RGMI Press
Temple Hills, Maryland
www.rgminternational.org

Cover design by Fletcher Maffett.

Photos courtesy of the author.

ISBN: 978-1-7324287-1-3

Library of Congress Control Number: 2019903313

10 9 8 7 6 5 4 3 2

1. Self-Help. 2. Self-Discovery. 3. Self-Empowerment.
4. Faith and Fire. 5. Strategies for Success.

Source of paraphrased quote: Mike Lee, "Street Smarts" column,
FireRescue1.

PRINTED IN THE UNITED STATES OF AMERICA

 ACKNOWLEDGMENTS

First, I thank my mother, who gave her support and understanding of my desire to share my story. She is a woman of love, strength, courage, and style. Only she knows the untold stories of adversity that she endured for the love of her family. I salute her resilience and dignity.

I also thank my sisters, who gave their blessings as I took on the personal task of writing this book.

I am blessed to have had my father in my home and life, and I honor his memory. I thank God for our walk together and for the lessons learned.

I thank my daughters, who have listened to me retell parts of my story that are not always easy to hear. I appreciate their love and support, and the fact that they get to witness the humanness of their father.

Finally, I am blessed to have a wife who sees me for who I am today, and not for who I once projected myself to be. She has fed into me at times more than I sometimes deserve. Her love and support cannot be matched.

CONTENTS

FOREWORD

Having known the author for nearly 40 years, I am very proud of Roderick Mitchell's accomplishments as a loving husband and father, respected first responder, much sought-after motivational speaker, and now an exceptional self-help guru. As a newly retired D.C. firefighter, he has written *Fire, Fury, Faith: A Story of Success by Fire* as a self-help book with wide appeal that speaks to the masses for achieving success. This book resonates with people seeking self-discovery, those intent on changing their lives, individuals in recovery, and people helping others to become their best selves.

Roderick likens getting through rough spots in life with fighting a raging fire—whether an internal firestorm or an external one. He draws parallels using the fire-fighting strategy and techniques that he learned at the beginning of his 28-year career as a first responder. While applying these techniques to everyday life experiences in a matter-of-fact way, Roderick invokes vivid images of the fireground with which he is intimately familiar and uses simple terminology that the reader will remember long after putting the book down.

Fire, Fury, Faith is both a self-help instructional guide and memoir. As a master motivational speaker, Roderick does not shy away from sharing his own pain of growing up in a home where alcohol-fueled domestic violence raged, and he is transparent about his personal struggle with alcoholism, coming to terms with his insecurities, and embarking on his own journey to healing, health, and wholeness.

It is through his transparency and authenticity that he earns the trust of the reader, as one who has successfully confronted obstacles to his personal development. He lays bare his life trajectory to encourage others needing to confront obstacles blocking their success. It is in this regard that Roderick explains the firefighting strategy, known as RECEO, and applies the techniques for putting out fires in our lives in a step-by-step process.

Roderick has walked the walk, and now he can talk about it openly and honestly to help others in challenging situations. *Fire, Fury, Faith* exhorts readers, in Roderick's own words, to "FINISH STRONG, FINISH STRONG, AND FINISH STRONG."

Jessica Cabness, Ph.D.
Licensed Clinical Social Worker-Certified
Largo, Maryland

INTRODUCTION: FIGHT FIRE LIKE A FIREFIGHTER

No doubt you have heard it is best to fight fire with fire. I love a good cliché. I often find truth at the heart of even the most hackneyed sayings. But after fighting dozens of fires, I have found that the advice to fight fire with fire is not exactly true.

I have spent three decades battling real fires as a career firefighter and EMT in Washington, D.C. Before that, I spent another 10 years battling personal firestorms to reach the brighter future I was convinced I could create for myself. What I learned about fighting fires in buildings and in my personal life—and what I will teach to you—is this: It is best to fight fire with firefighter methods.

Firefighters are professionals trained to fully understand that the best way to fight fire is with a proven strategy, tactical precision, a strong team that has your back, and a whole lot of water. We do not bring flamethrowers to a fire. We bring a hose with water flowing at just the right pressure and directed to just the right places to put out the fire. We also bring a big, loud truck and a strong team armed with just the right tools to get to wherever stubborn flames are and extinguish them.

This tactical, proven approach to fighting fire is true in everyday life just as it is true in everyday firefighting. If you have a fire to put out in your life, you can use these same winning strategies that firefighters use every day to conquer just about anything you are facing in life.

Since December 1990, I have battled fires on the frontlines in our nation's capital. I have tackled some of the worst fires that a firefighter can face. I have run into burning buildings on the verge of collapse with people trapped inside. I have fought the fires of fully engulfed structures in the sweltering heat of summer and in the brutal cold of winter. I know a thing or two about what it takes to battle a fire and come out alive and victorious.

Not so far from the blaze of real fires are often burns from real-life firestorms. The same skills and tactical know-how will make you a success at either (or both, if you happen to be an aspiring real-life firefighter).

Firefighters learn how to win against fires using tactical principles driven by methods and actions. The most established tactical approach is known in part as RECEO: Rescue, Expose, Confine, Extinguish, and Overhaul. I will teach you what these principles mean and how to use my life-adapted version of the RECEO principles to win against the fires blazing in your life. This approach works, whether you are facing personal firestorms that are raging out of control and need to be conquered, or if you have quietly burning hotspots that flare up from time to time that need to be contained until they can be put out for good—like a bad habit you just cannot seem to break.

When you have mastered my five RECEO-inspired principles of action, you will possess the strategies and the tactical know-how to conquer whatever fires are burning in your personal and professional life. Forget about fighting fire with fire. Learn how to fight fire with me.

CHAPTER 1:
WHAT IS RECEO?

The internal fire can be used to produce or destroy.
Redirect your fire of anger and pain into love and joy.
Learn to use your burning desire
for the development of yourself and others.
Be brave, be committed, be teachable—unleash your inner
firefighter for self-love and to serve another.

It is important to know that generations of firefighters have been trained to put out fires using tried and true, fundamental tactics. I have mentioned five principles thus far but the full firefighter's tactical training actually has seven principles: Rescue, Expose, Confine, Extinguish, Overhaul, Ventilate, Salvage. It is called "RECEO VS" for short.

In recent years, RECEO VS training has been adapted and modified for the "modern" firefighter. These new emerging trainings for professional first responders are still deeply rooted in the tactical RECEO principles. The acronyms and the order of the steps differ in the new trainings, but the approach is essentially the same.

In a later chapter, I will explain how you too can move fluidly between the steps of my program—even reorder the steps if you need to—and still adopt my approach with complete success. In my life-adapted version of firefighter tactical training, we focus on the first five principles because they are most relevant to personal and professional fires. They are the following:

- Rescue
- Expose
- Confine
- Extinguish
- Overhaul

If you have to apply VS—ventilate and salvage—when battling your real-life fires, then you have not mastered the five principles, and you need to go back to square one!

These terms refer to specific actions every first responder must take when facing any fire. When we take these same principles of action and apply them to our own lives, we become our own first responders capable of taking on and overcoming problems that once seemed impossible to beat. In effect, we become our very own first and best line of defense against all types of life threats, whether emotional, behavioral, relational, or financial.

The noted firefighting professional and trainer, Mike Lee, writing in the "Street Smarts" column of *FireRescue1* for firefighting professionals, captured this notion perfectly when he mentioned that not all tactics are needed at every fire, but they should always be a factor for consideration.

Each tactic can be delivered individually or in conjunction with another based on available resources and priority of completion in order to reduce the impact to the fireground.

In other words, every fire situation is unique. To battle a particular fire, you will not always need to use every tactic. But you have to assess the situation to know which tactics you need to use, and in which order you need to use them, to successfully put out the fire.

I believe deeply in this RECEO approach. I am committed to teaching it to you because it has been proven and it works—both on the fireground and in life.

Firefighting is equal parts bravery, commitment, and training. No one of these three aspects of firefighting is more important than the other. You must possess and nurture all three to succeed in fighting fires. You have to be brave enough to first want to fight fires and then to actually run into burning buildings when the time comes.

You have to be committed to your role on a team and as a leader. There is no room for big-headed egos on a well-functioning fire crew. Above all, you must be willing to learn from extensive training to ensure your success because unlike other professions, nobody is just born knowing how to best fight fires. Sure, there are parts of the job that are art and instinct, but mostly it is a science as well as a collection of learned skills.

Firefighters, like most of us in our careers and personal lives, are successful by demonstrating:

- effective communication skills
- integrity, composure, and a reassuring manner
- the ability to follow instructions
- the ability to work as part of a team
- problem-solving skills
- patience, understanding, and sensitivity
- confidence, strength, and resilience
- adaptability and flexibility

The first decade of my firefighting career was spent in one of the busiest firehouses in the city. Known as the "Castle by the Creek," Engine 27 (E-27) is a small, single company house with an ambulance. This is where I grew up in the fire department. Fires both big and small were not the only dangers and hazards of the big city firefighter. Prior to arriving at E-27, I had never seen a gunshot victim nor had experienced the sun rise so often. Located in the Northeast/Southeast sector of D.C., E-27 stayed on the go.

It was one of five firehouses in the then-eighth battalion. We averaged 20 runs every day while working a 24-hour shift. The calls involved everything, from the hurt fingernail, pained stomach, and headache to injuries and trauma resulting from fighting, stabbing, and gunshots. I witnessed two apparent suicidal hangings, and the complete burning of a middle-aged male stuck to the steering wheel of his flame-engulfed minivan. I truly became an emergency technician in what seemed at times like a war zone. It was not only a war between feuding groups of young men but a war of individuals fighting to survive in conditions that often appeared unfair, hazardous, and overwhelming.

The men and women in the then-eighth battalion of eight battalions in the city were known for carrying a heavy load. Nearly 50 percent of the calls were for fires, maybe for a two-story house or a multi-level apartment. Both created an adrenaline rush that called for one's full attention. Firefighting is physically demanding and draining. Depending upon the time of day, previous workload, weather conditions, and size of the fire, one hour on a "good" fire deserved a rest period of at least a few hours, which was never guaranteed! I can attest that the entire force of firefighters and EMTs throughout D.C. are introduced to absolutely superb training conducted by teams of experienced and highly skilled individuals.

As I look back on my days as a young "go-getter," I am thankful for my initial training at the academy, the ongoing drills to reinforce my skills, and the on-the-job training that could not be beat. I am forever grateful for the tradition of teamwork that remains alive and well throughout the firefighting family.

As a veteran firefighter, I can also tell you that experience and on-the-job training deepen your bravery, commitment, and learning. In other words, you get better and better at them the more you do them. Think of aging like fine wine or anything else that gets better over time.

The more fires you fight, the more experienced you become with applying the firefighting techniques. Even when you do not succeed at putting out a fire the first time, you are learning and getting better. And you draw on your experience to go back again and attack any lingering hidden little fires (in the firefighting business, we sometimes call these "hotspots").

You may be thinking to yourself: *I don't have the skills or the knowledge of how to fight these life threats on my own. If I did, they wouldn't be threats!*

The fact of the matter is that most of us are already equipped with the tools needed to confront and conquer most challenges or firestorms in our lives. We just need training to unlock and develop our own skills to unleash our inner firefighter.

This is not to say that professional help might not be in order for some of life's most difficult challenges. At some point, most of us turn to professional support in the form of doctors, therapists, clergy, coaches, mentors, or other support systems to help get us through the toughest situations. I am not suggesting that you replace the professional support you may feel you need. Instead, I encourage you to think of professional support as a complement and a catalyst to the support you first provide for yourself.

It is almost time to dive into my life-adapted RECEO program to understand exactly how you translate five firefighting concepts into real-life strategies for successfully battling life's firestorms step-by-step when you commit to Rescue, Expose, Confine, Extinguish, and Overhaul. Before we start, I want to take a moment to think about my life before I became a firefighter and emergency medical technician. I knew nothing about the tactics that firefighters use to take out a fire. And to be honest, I did not start off knowing how to fight for my life.

My childhood was marked with setbacks and scarred by my choices as a result of my inability to preemptively control negative life sparks that morphed into blazes. One bad choice would lead to the next, and small issues were gassed into becoming bigger ones. I could have participated in more uplifting and edifying opportunities, had I followed my parents' directions instead of running on self-will. I immersed myself into the party life with family and friends—a life that later became less about fun and more about emotional distress and thoughts of suicide. I felt that dying was easier than living. My life had to change!

CHAPTER 2:
LITTLE RODGIE—
WHERE IT ALL
BEGAN

I was a little fellow born with a spirit of kindness and the willingness to help the underdog. My thick, fiery red hair was short and styled into a mini Afro that would never grow. As a child of the 1960s and 1970s, I was heavily influenced by the classic television sitcoms of the "perfect" families—*The Brady Bunch, Father Knows Best, The Dick Van Dyke Show,* and *Dennis the Menace.*

Roderick is my full first name. How it became Rodgie, I will never know. I had no outstanding athletic abilities nor early signs of academic prowess. I was just an average kid wanting to find peace and joy within myself and within the environment around me. Hidden behind my smile were growing feelings of fear, pain, anger, and confusion.

I always felt the need for more attention than I ever received, especially from my father. My focus was to seek attention—the type of attention and time that I imagine a stay-at-home parent can give to a child. Both of my parents worked to provide a comfortable lifestyle for our family. I never went hungry, and had mostly every game, toy, or sneaker I wanted. But the things I lacked most were self-esteem and self-assurance—the type of assurance from a loving parental source that helps a kid feel that he is OK just as he is.

My social and behavioral issues were highlighted as early as the first grade. I struggled throughout all of my schooling. I found myself daydreaming away most of the school day while sitting at my desk and scratching the plaque off my unbrushed teeth. My mother would wake me for school and send me into the bathroom to bathe, but I would turn on the bath faucet and let the water run as I sat on the toilet catching up on my sleep. I learned much later that poor personal hygiene in a child can be early signs of depression (or of simply being an eight-year-old boy).

I often admit to myself that my struggles in school were not a direct reflection of my mental capabilities. The obstacles I faced related more to a fight to focus while detaching myself from the distractions at home and the world around me. I wanted to escape the pain of arguments and fights at home so when the school day ended, my daydreaming continued.

I was about eight years old when I sat at the breakfast table in our new apartment on Belleview Street in Southeast Washington, D.C. The Linda Pollin apartment complex spanned several acres with hundreds of apartments over several four-story and five-story buildings. Linda Pollin Apartments were named in honor of the daughter of the then-named Washington Bullets basketball team owner, who was Abe Pollin.

One morning, my one and only older brother felt the need to hassle me while I attempted to eat my breakfast. This was not unusual for him but for some reason, which I cannot remember, he really got under my skin that day. With no thought of the repercussions, I picked up my fork and threw it at him. The fork flew across the table and stuck neatly and dangerously into his forehead. I would think that I had received the whipping of my life because of it, but I really do not remember. We both survived, and that simply became a story we infrequently share with others to this day. That act of anger was a glimpse of what lay deep inside me.

I had two very good friends that I spent most of my playtime with. One was Jimmie, who was "the other guy" as it related to our girlfriend Barbara, who would "go with" me one week, only to quit me and become Jimmie's girlfriend the next week. This went on the entire four to five years my family lived at Linda Pollin Apartments. Barbara was a pretty brown girl with soft, curly brown hair that twisted into long ponytails. She was not only pretty to me but also to other little boys in the neighborhood.

This created a problem for me, not only with Jimmie but with a little neighborhood "thug" who wanted me to let go of the love of my eight-year-old life and let him slide in on my girl.

I experienced all of these situations after the landmark passing of the *Brown v. Board of Education* case, back when African American kids were being bussed to white neighborhood schools for the purpose of social mixing and equal educational opportunities. In third grade, I would travel by bus from in front of Draper Elementary School in Southeast—a few blocks away from my apartment—to Hardy Elementary, located in a very wealthy area of Northwest.

The thug and his boys waited outside of Draper every school day, ready to pounce on me and convince me to cut ties with my girl. I remember being afraid and anxious as the bus pulled onto the street for drop off. As soon as the door popped open, I would shift into fifth gear and run home, nonstop. There were times I risked being hit by moving vehicles because "Ole' Jack Rabbit Rod" was not about to get caught and engage in hand-to-hand combat with the thug and his boys—until one day when I finally stood up for myself and faced him. As it turned out, I came out on top! *Whew, what a relief*, I thought to myself. After that, I had no more trouble with him but confrontation was still not something I easily dealt with.

Outside of my heartbreak and fight for my girl, most memories of Linda Pollin were good. My best friend Dion and I would sit on our toy trucks and ride down a big dirt hill near our apartment. Our parents and siblings spent a lot of time together as though we all were related. Maybe that was the result of living in such close proximity. I noticed that others with similar values and interests who lived above or below one another related as though they were family. Those were the good old days!

Linda Pollin was the third apartment location my family lived in before making the move to our first single family house at 418 Emerson Street in Northwest. It was a four-bedroom house with a basement, placed in the middle of a long row of similarly built brick homes. A feeling of excitement came along with the new school, new friends, and new adventures.

As I look back, Emerson Street is where everything inside and outside of the home progressed. I remember riding in the back of my friend's family station wagon where his father would pack my buddy and three of his closest friends and then head to Charles Town Raceway in West Virginia. My buddy's father liked to bet on the horses and the boys simply enjoyed the long ride, food, and sights of the big, handsome, muscular creatures tamed to carry a featherweight human around a mile-length track at amazing speeds.

I attended Barnard Elementary, my new neighborhood school, from grades four through six. My anger was hard to manifest when it came time for me to stand up for myself against my constant bully, Marvin. Marvin was dark-skinned, mean, and intimidating. I was convinced back in the day that the darker a person was—especially a black male—the meaner and more prone to violence he was.

I dreaded being in the lunch line to have Marvin approach me and spew that famous line I heard too often from the bully: "Got any money? All I find, I can have!" It was sort of a question and a demand at the same time! He would take my lunch money and a few times punched me in the face, either before or afterward.

I think I came close to getting my butt whipped as an adult because my ego and pride would not let me back down and accept that behavior. I would tell myself, *I don't have to take that anymore.* I would stand in stubborn resolve, even if I was scared to death and the odds were not in my favor. Be careful of allowing your past to dictate your future thinking and behavior.

One time I tried to use Marvin's same bullying style against Reggie, a little chubby school buddy who wore braces and seemed harmless and playful like me. I have vague memories of me trying to shuffle Reggie around but, unlike me, he fought back. I do not think we actually locked horns. He simply did not back down, and that was pretty much the end of my bullying career.

I believe even before being bullied, my natural inclination and spirit was to always fight for the underdog. Yes, I know that my bully record was not very good with the story of my buddy Reggie, but bullying was just not in me. Reggie would not take it anyway, so we went back to being mutual friends—he, the little chubby guy with braces and glasses, and me, the redheaded kid who was simply trying to make it through a day without getting punched in the lip.

My father was a hardworking man who was born and raised in the small town of Lake Waccamaw, North Carolina, which is outside of Wilmington. His breakfasts were fit for a king, and he would make a mean plate of grits, scrambled eggs with spring onions, biscuits, and a choice of pork breakfast meats. He cooked dinner and was talented on the grill as well. My father's industry and job as an offset pressman was taken over by emerging print technologies. My mother was also a hardworking woman who was born and raised in Washington, D.C. As his wife and mother of five, she would take on the responsibilities of a full-time job. I remember my mother being the grocer and the cook. I was blessed with having two parents who knew their way around the kitchen. They were good-looking people, too. My mother is pretty, well-kept, and classy. My father was a handsome guy plucked from the lighter side of the black race.

Most households I knew were comprised of two parents who both worked for the family. By the age of 12, I had two working parents, siblings, and a couple of dogs. One was a silver and white German Shepherd named Wendy, and the other was Skippy, a small, tan Cocker Spaniel. My friend Timmie had a stay-at-home mom, which was unheard of in my neck of the woods. Right around the corner from Emerson Street was Delafield Street. That block of families did not appear as well off as the families on Emerson.

My own little room was painted my favorite color, blue. I was in my own world, as were my siblings in their spaces. My oldest sister Darletta had moved to live with my maternal grandmother by that time. My next oldest sister, Tasha, was a high schooler and growing up fast. My youngest sister Crystal, who is hearing impaired, was locked out of most conversations in the household. I know for sure that none of us had a world so much of our own as Crystal. She has been hearing impaired since soon after birth. While everyone in the house could easily hear and talk to one another, that was not the case for her.

I look back and think about how selfish and self-centered I was in regard to not thinking to include Crystal in all our conversations. Certainly, as children we usually stay in an "it's all about me" mode of thinking and reasoning. I am grateful that she attended grammar and high school on the campus of Gallaudet University, a well-known school for the deaf in Washington, D.C. Crystal also had a strong core of friends. I can remember how she gathered with them in the living room as they communicated amongst one another using sign language. Their hand movements, finger speed, and facial gestures when communicating were fascinating to watch. Being a guy who loves the expression of emotion, drama, and sound that comes with a passion-filled conversation, I have always enjoyed watching a group conversation being held as I enjoyed the fact that I was the outsider looking in. Far too often the shoe was on the other foot, and Crystal must have felt like the outsider looking in time and time again.

She and I are closest in age so that meant we would often find ourselves together at home needing to communicate. Therefore, I chose to at least learn to sign the alphabet of the American Sign Language system. I have learned some basic one-word gestures beyond the alphabet but not much. Today when we are gathered together as a family, I appoint myself as the group interpreter, although I would not make it as an interpreter for a living. You could equate the speed of my sign language to the speed of a sloth. By the time I have finished spelling a word, or have my sister teach me a new gesture, or remind me of one I forgot, the sun has risen and set. But I try.

My sister teases me because I have been saying that I am going to get better but my better has not come. I am glad I have become more conscious of including her in group conversations. I have no idea what her personal journey as a deaf citizen has been like but I am reminded of how much I love her and how proud I am of her as a mother and self-sufficient woman. I know her road has not been easy, and I bow to honor the hurdles of life that she has overcome.

I believe that the summer before my entry into junior high was when all hell broke loose at home. My friends and I made go-karts from scrap wood and wheels removed from stolen shopping carts belonging to a local grocery store. We would each have one and race down the middle of our street speeding, spinning, and braking with the help of good old-fashioned Chuck Taylor All Star high-top sneakers. Those were the days when a mother would come to the front door and yell for her children to come in from a day full of fun, adventurous, creative, enterprising, and sometimes smelly outdoor activities.

By age 13, I was in full swing of traveling down the road of sex, drugs, and R&B. I always wanted to grow up fast. I started smoking Kool cigarettes, which I thought aligned with the image of coolness I tried so hard to project. After Kool cigarettes, I moved on to a milder brand of menthols in Newport cigarettes, then to a third brand of cigarettes that were a slimmer, milder version of a cigar and cigarette mixed. The "follower" in me tried to keep up with my brother and older cousins, and commercial advertising presented the smokes as looking really cool, fun, and flavorful.

After several years of trying to find the coolest, best-tasting cigarettes, I settled into smoking Newport and marijuana. I thought that I had really graduated; I believed that I could not be cool without being high at the same time.

I could not wait to engage in sexual activity. Actually, I tried my best not to wait. Any neighborhood girl near my age would be in my sights. Stacy was the sister of my friend Donnie, and I made several attempts to kiss and rub up against her in the dark, on the porch, and behind the porch furniture! They were all unsuccessful attempts at doing something I was ill-equipped to handle, but I was anxious to try.

I had made my way into MacFarland Junior High in Northwest, where education was nowhere on my radar. The party was on, and so was the slow decline into my personal hell.

While in the seventh grade, I lived with my father and brother during a period when my parents were separated. I failed my first year in middle school and the thought of giving up was planted. I lacked interest and discipline as it pertained to school. My urge to run from those old feelings of inadequacy were stronger than a desire or plan to invest in a future worth working toward.

By the time my parents had reconciled, I had repeated seventh grade, so I was on my way to Catholic school. During my first few days there, I overheard a classmate threatening to "whoop the ass" of another. I had guessed that the only difference between Catholic school and public school was the word Catholic. I spent my second seventh grade year in St. Peter Catholic School on Capitol Hill, enjoying early dismissal on Wednesdays and eating Roy Rogers cheeseburgers on the way home from school.

That was the year I played organized basketball for the first time. I was a back-up on the junior varsity team. I never have been much of a "baller," which as a black male in the inner city who grew to nearly six feet tall was not cool. But it just was not my thing. I played organized baseball while living on Emerson Street with a local recreation center, and I was a member of the Little League Pittsburgh Pirates. Both were short-lived careers. Organized sports was not a big part of my childhood.

The boys in the neighborhood did get together and play different styles of football. We played tag football in the middle of the street, marking the distance between two parked cars as the playing field and having to stop playing each time neighborhood traffic needed to get by. We would get mad when adults yelled at us for hitting their cars with the ball. As an adult, I can now completely understand their position. I would have definitely been one of those fussing adults. Seeing kids playing in the street is not something I see much of anymore. While the street is not the safest environment for play, I believe outdoor activity is positive and physically nurturing for developing children.

We played tackle football on the grass of the perimeter of Barnard Elementary, which did not have a football field. Sometimes we chose teams, and other times we would play "throw up tackle," one of our favorites. It was every man for himself. The entire group of boys gathered together as the football was thrown in the air. Whoever caught it was the one offensive player while everyone else was on defense. The one runner had to evade every boy on the field as we all aimed to tackle that one runner. We would go home tired and hungry, with dirty jeans and dirty faces! At my house, a personal favorite appetizer would consist of a few hot dogs with melted cheese and a glass of milk. Those were the good old days!

I was held back in the first and seventh grades, and I barely made it out of the ninth grade. I went to my one and only prom, and I had attended seven different schools while barely maintaining a 2.0 grade point average during my entire school career. I was capable, and had I not had an unhealthy mental perspective and a lack of freedom to think and feel good about myself and my environment, I believe my social and academic capabilities would have matched those of the average student. Due to the stresses and worries of home, it was there that I learned to internalize my thoughts: *I am not good enough. I am not smart enough. I am not worth it.*

It was enough to cause me to give up on me. I could walk, run, jump, and swim like all the other normal kids. But my number one disability was my lack of belief and placing value in Roderick.

In addition, my story was one of alcoholism, which resulted in mental, emotional, and behavioral deficiencies. I am the fourth of five children who I think have all dealt with the pains of growing up as children of an alcoholic father. Technically, it is not my position to diagnose my father as such, but based on my personal experience and by eventually admitting my alcoholism, I think most—if not all medical, social, or therapeutic professionals—would have diagnosed my father with the disease of alcoholism.

Be Brave, Be Committed, Be Teachable
It is time to begin to unleash your inner firefighter! You will learn the Rescue principle in the next chapter, which delves into step 1 of the proven RECEO principles.

CHAPTER 3:
RESCUE

I am rescuing myself from the fires of strife
blazing in my personal and professional life.

The first concept is Rescue. Unlike what you may be imagining, and certainly not what you have been led to believe from television dramas about first responders, Rescue is not blindly running into a blazing building to save fire victims who may not even exist. Rescue actually involves sizing up the fireground scene, talking quickly with witnesses, and determining if there is a need for Rescue.

In your personal life, this concept works in a similar way. You carefully size up your problem and decide what type of Rescue is required, if any. In life, unlike in real firegrounds, there is usually a need for Rescue. Why? Because the personal firestorms you are facing are often not of your own doing, at least in part. For most people, this first principle is probably the toughest part of my approach and is also where I often encounter the most resistance.

People are not inclined to look at themselves as the root of their own dysfunction. It is much easier—and much more convenient—to place the blame on other people: your spouse or companion, your family, your business partner, the people who bullied you, the hard knocks you barely survived growing up. It is much easier to blame any one of these people and circumstances instead of taking personal responsibility, even if it was all beyond your control.

"Life does not give you what you want, it gives you what you are. You are bold, you are rich, you are deserving of a life beyond your imagination." -RKM

I have come to understand that it was not my father's fault, nor was it my mother's fault, nor was it my fault. Unfortunately, the stories of family struggles and misfortunes live in every part of America and beyond, and none of these individuals is at fault. This is not about blame; this is about freedom! Are there responsible individuals and parties? Yes! Did my mother purposely marry a man for the purpose of physical, emotional, mental, and spiritual abuse? No! Did my father purposely grow up as a child in a household where these same issues may have abounded? He had no choice in his position of birth and early childhood environment. Quite frankly, he and I never talked about his childhood. He has since died, thus I may never discover the details of the little boy who became "that" man to me.

Forgiveness

At the age of 21, my mother and my father had separated and divorced. My relationship with my father afterward included an unspoken understanding that what we experienced as a family was in the past and forever done. We never talked about the horrors and results of those nights—the feelings of fear, shame, guilt, and anger that carried into the mornings after and years beyond that. He was not a man who spoke about his feelings or his personal flaws as a person. But I know in his heart that he loved his children and did the best he knew how.

As part of a personal development training nearly 20 years after the day I stood up to him, protecting my mother from another angry attack, I was urged to give him a call to offer my hand and heart in forgiveness. I spoke briefly of the past episodes and offered my forgiveness for his actions and their negative emotional impact upon me. He very nonchalantly responded that he was happy for me.

Yes, just as you might be confused by that response, so was I. What I learned from his answer is that the act of forgiving really is not about the other person. It is almost completely about you. If we truly forgive and "let it go," then we are free—free to move on in every area of our lives, growing beautifully and courageously, into a better and brighter future for ourselves and those we love. May God bless the life and spirit of Steadman A. Mitchell.

We all respond differently in some of the same situations. Oftentimes in the Rescue of yourself, it is not all about, or even mostly about, what you experienced or who inflicted something upon you. It is about how you reacted, how you internalized your reactions, and how you have gotten stuck in a cycle of self-harm based on your reactions.

It is hard for most people to realize, and even harder to accept, that when Rescue is properly performed, you are not rescuing yourself from shadowy outside forces. In most cases, those forces vanished long ago. Instead, you are rescuing yourself from the only danger still present and stoking the flames of your personal fires. You are delivering yourself from the thing that keeps you trapped in the bad habits or the self-destructive behaviors.

Reflection for Rescue
You are going to rescue yourself from yourself—from the fires yet blazing in your personal and professional life causing the war within yourself, such as:

- pornographic addiction
- gambling addiction
- street or prescription drug addiction
- alcohol addiction
- cigarette addiction
- cell phone/tablet addiction
- food addiction
- work addiction
- shopping addiction

- sexual addiction
- abuse and neglect
- codependent behaviors
- divorce and separation
- job loss and dissatisfaction
- relationship breakup
- low self-esteem
- depression

At the root of all these ailments are feelings of fear and inadequacy. Often, we feel that we are not equipped with the capabilities to deal with life's many situations. Rescue is an introspective experience that calls for honesty and readiness.

"Practice random acts of trust, courage, and faith.
Believe in yourself." -RKM

If you are not up to that task right away, it is OK. Most of us are not. The good thing is that you can execute the other tactics and come back to this one. But in the end, you will always have to come back to this one. No firefight is ever successful when victims in need of Rescue are ignored. This is especially true of the fires you fight in your own life.

Rescue tackles four important questions:

1. How did I get here?
2. What was the cost?
3. Was it/is it worth it?
4. How can I participate in the process?

You must reflect on the parts of the past that have created your current state of fear, fantasy, and stagnation. In doing so, you truly begin the Rescue process. You must ask yourself questions that open your mind and heart to the reality of your current state and the possibilities in improving yourself. This is what I had to do to get sober and start a new way of living.

More questions to ask yourself:

1. Were my choices worth it?
2. What has it cost me, financially, mentally, physically, spiritually, and/or emotionally?
3. How can I take the lead and full responsibility for the reclaiming of my life?
4. What kinds of choices do I need to make to progress?
5. Do I surround myself with safe, supportive, and encouraging people?
6. How do I continuously engage myself in personal development?
7. Is my self-talk a healthy and positive inner conversation, or is it opposite of that?

When we gain the courage to ask these questions and search for the answers is when we have become the lead rescuer in the healing and reinvention of our lives.

You must take stock of your environment. On the scene of a fire emergency, the firefighter's number one priority is to implement an effective and efficient plan of action that provides a means of egress for themselves and/or any possible victims. This same concept can also be used to bring attention to the individual or group by making them aware of the part they can play in the rescue, redevelopment, and enhancement of their lives. You must make wise lifestyle choices and raise your level of personal commitment to conscientious community awareness of self and others.

Success with Rescue

If you are to succeed in my program, then Rescue, fully undertaken and executed, is vital. The key to your own successful Rescue mission is your participation in the process. It is the only way to achieve it. You have to be fully present and, in fact, take leadership and ownership for your own deliverance from your past way of unhealthy thinking, old bad habits, and self-destructive behaviors. As you change, the old ways of thinking and behaving will not serve you well and will actually become foreign to you.

The Truth

It is important to recognize and acknowledge the role you have played in your life's situations. There comes a time when we can no longer blame other people, places, or events for our current state. Rescue is the beginning of taking full responsibility for your stuff. Yes, at different times you were not in control of several events that happened in your life. As children, of course we were at the mercy of the adults and other guardians and influential figures in our lives. As we grew and entered into adulthood, we found ourselves lugging mental and emotional baggage—wanted and unwanted collectibles of uncertainty and pain—along with us.

CHAPTER 4:
EXPOSE

While exposing old realities
I take steps forward courageously.
When I live in bare truth, I can see
Myself as victim yet victor getting freed.

When executing the fireground tactic of expose, the firefighters work to uncover hidden dangers and protect surrounding structures from the heat and flames of the building at hand. As we fight fires in our lives, our challenge to Expose is a little different, but closely related to the firefighting tactic.

Our goal in life is to be transparent with ourselves and lay bare all of our issues. To do this, we must be introspective by thinking and reflecting on things we have kept hidden from everyone, including ourselves. We must apply Expose to feelings and thinking that are contradictory to living a healthy and productive life. Willingness and honesty are key to the act of being truly introspective. I have found that Expose, or exposure, is easier said than done, much like Rescue.

Wait a minute, you say? I just asked you to tackle the principle of Rescue and now I am telling you to lay bare, as in naked and vulnerable? *Surely staying fully covered when battling the fire is essential,* you argue. After all, the firefighters show up in full regalia of protective gear.

Why should you be asked to lay bare? Before you shut down and give up—before you resign to thinking this RECEO thing is not for you—I submit to you that the concept of Expose is critical to the successful firefight. Right here, in this moment of Expose, you are both the firefighter and the potential fire victim (remember, ultimately you are rescuing yourself). The fire victim is the most vulnerable figure on the fireground, and it is no different in real-life firestorms.

"Most people are afraid of the fire on the outside, when it is the untamed fire on the inside that kills the spirit of faith, love, and beauty." -RKM

There is a connection we all share as people with family facing struggles that create pain, anger, and frustration, which often translates into mental and emotional anguish. Through my struggle, I learned to look within and around me for the strength, guidance, and love that would carry me through each day. We discover the power of love through sharing and connecting with others who have experienced similar trials, sometimes connecting with people of unlikely similarities.

Quite often throughout my upbringing, my father's mood determined the temperature of our home environment. While I do remember happy times of family connection, home was often scary, painful, disturbing, and traumatic. My father had a temper that turned him red with anger.

Unfortunately, the trauma deriving from domestic violence in our home had a long-lasting negative impact on me. I was an emotional basket case who was scared of my own shadow. I prayed for peace amongst all human beings. With the prevalence of war around the world, the fight for civil rights among African Americans in these United States baffled me. The marginalized social status of black people was enough to paint my young mind with a brush of hopelessness and despair that remained for decades.

The intensity of the abuse that I witnessed at home created a depth of fear in my 10-year-old psyche that I fight to erase and replace with love to this day—the kind of love that every child needs to feel whole and complete—the type of nurturing love from a parent that lets a kid know that they are worth fighting for. It is the attending to a child's needs that supports and builds the child up from his heart to the smile of happiness on his face.

Throughout all of my outdoor play, road trips with my core group of friends, and chasing girls, I carried the feelings of fear, inadequacy, and shame with me everywhere I went. Sometimes I was uncertain of how the night would go when my father arrived home. As I think back, it seems as though most of his tirades occurred on weekends, perhaps because he was too tired to raise hell after a day of work during the workweek.

Some of the uglier fights etched in my mind happened after coming home from a family outing. One of the most unusual characteristics of the mornings after these nights of total horror was the silence that ensued. Nobody spoke of the hell that we all endured the night before. My father acted as though nothing happened, and things slowly went back to "our" normal. But even when I walked out of my house, I sometimes felt alone, lost, hurt, and confused. When I think back on those days, I am amazed at how well I have done to create a generally happy life for myself.

Around the time that I entered sixth grade, my friends and I began to "wanna be like the big boys" and drink alcohol. It started with small amounts of beer and wine. I can remember standing outside of a liquor store in a small shopping strip of storefront businesses. There was a record shop, a laundromat, and a cleaners. My buddies and I would scan the customers going in and out of the liquor store and then we would wait to ask the most likely person if they would buy us a bottle of wine. At that time, I believe we were drinking Boones Farm. Most times, we succeeded in finding a young male of legal drinking age to accept our change and help us buy the poison that we believed would elevate us from boys to men.

That was the typical scenario for us inner-city boys whom you would see walking to the nearest corner store and hanging around there. Unfortunately, millions of us do not make it off that corner. The escape from my reality of pain, fear, low self-esteem, and confusion began as what seemed to be fun in a wine bottle. At nearly age 36, for me it ended with practically the same emotions and feelings of inadequacy, only in adult-sized portions which felt reckless, overwhelming, and soul-crushing.

After 21 years of family trauma, my ability to cope had been thwarted and my ability to think through the hell flames I survived was derailed. After witnessing the man I loved to the core of my being turn from a caring, hardworking father and husband into someone I trembled to see, it negatively affected me for several years to follow.

Until the age of 21, I was unable to rationalize these horrific events that occurred again and again in my young life. When finally at the age of 21, I was able to defend my mother from my father, who would show up in a fit of untamed fiery anger. That would be my father's last attempt of physical aggression upon my mother. Over the next two decades, my life would take many turns before getting to the period of exhaustion, ultimate fear, and confusion.

At age 19, I was barely able to care for myself when I was told I would be a father. After a broken heart and much anguish, the relationship with my daughter's mother ended, leaving me with no desire for romantic love. We were two young people engaging in real adult activity; I for one know that I was not ready for the responsibility of helping to raise a child.

For the next 20 years, my life would be full of ups and downs, with other women that I would form strong connections, and a near-marriage. The woman I almost married agreed that had we gotten married, there was a strong possibility that the marriage would have ended in divorce. I was immature, lacking the personal development and commitment to nurture a lasting, healthy marriage.

Some say hell is after death. I suggest to you that if you have ever wanted to commit suicide because you felt your life was not worth living, as I once felt, you know something about living in hell on earth. When your spirit is broken, the other aspects of your humanity are incapacitated, non-functioning. My life was a constant question of *How can I fix me? Why am I broken?* I looked for someone or something outside of me to put me back together.

What I discovered was that putting the pieces of me back together starts with me being willing to look in the mirror, face my fears, accept the good (healthy) and the bad (unhealthy) parts of who I am.

My early dysfunction was enough to cause me to give up on me. I could walk, run, jump, and swim like all the other normal kids. But like I said earlier, my number one disability was my lack of belief and placing value in Roderick. I stumbled and fell many times before I found my way.

My self-esteem took a brutal hit because of the regular, scary, and painful verbal and physical altercations. I came to understand that my parents loved us tremendously to the best of their ability. I was mentally and emotionally behind my chronological age by 5 to 10 years at any given time, which would slowly match my behavior and life-coping skills with that of the 57-year-old man I would one day become.

Later in life, I learned the importance of meditation and how to become introspective by reading dozens of personal development books. I literally devoured every bit of knowledge I could about how to build a better, stronger, more confident, and balanced version of myself. I wanted a stable foundation upon which to build a strong future.

Firefighting was nowhere on my radar at the time of the call from my oldest sister, Darletta. Sometime in 1989, she said to me, "Hey Lil' Bro, I heard on the radio that the fire department is hiring."

There I was, a 28-year-old high school dropout who had gotten my GED 4 years after I quit school. Regardless, I was considered a good and reliable employee by my managers at work, and I had little to no thoughts or desires of working my way up. The seed of greatness was born in me, as with us all, at birth—but my experiences and interpretation of them left me disconnected from most of the possibilities associated with success and greatness.

I was not too far into my formal training to become a firefighter when I first noticed the striking similarities between firefighting tactical response and the tactical strategies needed to rebuild a life. It was as though fires in a building and fires in personal life were not all that different from one another. But it would take me more than two decades before I decided to adapt the formal firefighting tactics into a program to fight life's fires.

My life and its lessons would take many turns before reaching the point of exhaustion, fear, and dysfunction. After drinking alcohol for nearly 25 years, I was physically ill, mentally unstable, and emotionally depressed. The feelings of desperation, of dying, and of wanting to live and thrive were overwhelming. I surrendered my will and my understanding of how my life was going or not going for me by voluntarily entering a 12-step program. Once I did that, every aspect of my being gradually changed to my benefit.

Now that I have retired from firefighting after 28 years, I feel like my firefighting work is not ending. In fact, it is just getting started. From this point forward, I will be able to devote all of my time to teaching others how to fight life's fires with proven strategies. My goal now is to share with as many people as I can all of the lessons and tactics I learned and mastered during 40 years of fighting fires of my own—in life and as a career firefighter.

Finding my way also consisted of cobbling together a set of tools that helped me rebuild my life better than I could have imagined. I achieved (and still maintain) sobriety with the help of that 12-step program. I have been sober for over 20 years. To fight the agony and pain that I was trying to escape in the first place, I used other tools. I learned how to confront my innermost feelings and find personal healing through a combination of reflection, physical fitness, and transforming my life to be healthy in mind and body.

When battling a blaze, firefighters look for exposures, which are areas inside and outside of the structure where a fire has an opportunity to spread rapidly and get out of control. Staying ahead of the fire requires a good firefighter to artfully "read" smoke and skillfully manage or expose the exposures.

The goal of identifying and getting ahead of exposures is to establish lines of containment for a progressing fire. In other words, managing exposures is how you start to get control of the fire.

This really happened, and I lived to tell about it.
I want to share a crazy story that taught me some valuable lessons—mainly that sometimes we are simply not in

control of situations we face. We can only be prepared to be used for good at all times.

On a bright, summer Friday afternoon in Washington, D.C., I paid a visit to my then-girlfriend's apartment. I remember it was August 22, 1986. Her sister was visiting from North Carolina, along with the sister's two small boys and a third sister's seven-year-old daughter.

I knocked on the apartment door and the seven-year-old answered. She recognized me through my association with her aunt. She opened the door, giving no indication of what lurked behind it. We greeted and as I proceeded into the living room area, a slim man with whom I was not familiar walked toward me. We passed one another, each without acknowledging the other.

After I took a couple steps past him, I was attacked from behind. He violently assaulted me with two deep stab wounds into each side of my upper back. He stabbed me once more in the upper right arm as I attempted to defend myself by grabbing him and throwing him to the floor. In a span of time that seemed like an eternity, I began to critically bleed and I felt the loss of strength and fight. As I held his wrist with the loosening grip of my bloody hands, the 8-inch knife was less than an inch from the tip of my nose. As our struggle continued, he was as anxious as I was to end this battle, which had foiled his demonic act of intrusion and rape.

Just before a mutual release of his intent to put his tool of death through my face and my release of his wrists, I heard a scream from the master bedroom, which led me to believe there was a second assailant holding the visiting sister. After running down eight flights of stairs bleeding heavily from the torso and feeling respiratory distress from a punctured lung, I made my way to the bottom floor.

I am forever grateful to the unknown civilian, who no longer waited for the city ambulance to arrive and rushed my bloody body to the nearest hospital in her private vehicle instead. That day is forever sealed in my mind and spirit as a day of lessons and blessings. I believe strongly that I was used as an instrument to help save the woman who had been raped, gagged, and tied in the bedroom of the apartment I visited that day.

I have thought about the emotional harm done to the children as they witnessed this gruesome, near-death experience. I also pray for the sister's physical, mental, and emotional wellbeing after such an inhumane, cruel, and vicious experience.

My ability to physically withstand the stabbing and hard-fought tussle along the perimeter of the apartment is attributed to my Taekwondo training at the time, and of course the grace of a loving God who had more in store for my life. The awareness of a loving God did not come until later in my life. It took more life experiences to affect my spiritual, mental, physical, and emotional wellbeing, to be able to appreciate the fact that I am not always in control of my every outcome. Intention, and above all grace, work hand in hand. Since that day, for me to say,

"God, use me as You will" has a new and more profound meaning.

I left the hospital three days later with a scarred body and mind, determined to not allow that horrific experience change how I engage my fellow man. It was not overnight but eventually the natural lover of peace in me began to shine its way through. No matter the images and judgments that flash through my mind or the uninterested strangers I come across, I make the conscious decision to always work toward positive engagement with everyone I encounter. The bloodshed from that hot summer day could blanket my eyes with the stifling emotions of both fear and anger. Instead, I make the conscious effort to speak to the quiet, smile in the presence of frowns, and remain hopeful among the hopeless.

Reflection for Expose

I once heard it said that a person is as sick as his or her secrets. What we hold inside can either feed us or kill us. Holding onto damaging thoughts that translate to depressive feelings and destructive behaviors cause illness on every level.

The principle of Expose tackles all available negative obstacles that we need to let go of. Negative thoughts or resentments that come from past hurt and pain, as well as some actions that were put on us by others that we have consciously and unconsciously accepted, can adversely affect our progress of personal ascent. Actions that negatively affect our esteem and emotional balance must be addressed.

"Feed the stomach and you will be full for a while. Feed the soul and you will be full for a lifetime." -RKM

Otherwise, we live anywhere between a mildly to severely confused state, choosing to make confusing life decisions from this perspective instead of living our lives in a state of harmony. We find ourselves maladjusted and struggling to find peace, happiness, and balance. We exist in states of emotional pain, mental anguish, and personal disappointment. We yearn to be rid of unproductive thoughts and emotions that stifle and restrain us from breaking through to a life of sunlit hope and clarity.

Success with Expose

Executing the action principle of Expose will help you to uncover:

- negative thoughts
- negative emotions
- anger at self
- pain
- confusion
- disappointment with self and others

The action principle of Expose has two vital functions that involve protection and enlightenment.

1. **Protect your outside exposures.** In this case, your exposures are family, friends, and associates who have a genuine concern for your wellbeing.

2. **Clean your internal house.** When you become a better version of yourself, your light shines brighter with greater impact upon the people and situations you are involved with. This is achieved by exposing the negative mental stories of the past.

This exercise enables us to better love our family, friends, and others who have been pulling for us as we learn to better love ourselves. The principle of Expose is used to help you recognize the behaviors and thoughts from your past that perpetuate a negative pattern in the present. Self-examination, introspection, and honesty are key factors at this level. In your personal and professional life, this translates into better project management, improved service to others, and being more patient and understanding of your own process as well as the needs of others on your team.

The Truth

These are the stories that have shaped unhealthy patterns of selfish, self-loathing victimization. I write this from my personal experience. For years, I held onto the painful security of my past script—an old reality that I allowed to hang on way too long. This only changed when I made the decision to courageously take the steps of exposing my true feelings.

There is a sense of freedom when you can admit to yourself and to a trusting, non-judgmental confidant your story, along with any secrets that have held you in bondage. A major part of moving on is to expose the old negative thinking and habits that no longer serve you as you progress healthfully toward a positive and bright future, despite the positions that you face in life.

"You can only experience what you allow your mind to be open to. Step outside of the box of 'sameness.'" -RKM

Let us take a step that seems like a 180-degree turn. I just said that you need to seek the concept of Expose with a goal of being fully open and honest. Next, I am going to tell you that you have to confine and seal up, all while maintaining your Expose principles. Does this seem to be madness? I promise you that it will make complete sense, and you will have over half of the program under your belt when you learn how to apply the concept of Confine.

CHAPTER 5:
CONFINE

"Confine" is a state of mind.

If you think that fighting fires requires you to think outside the box, then this critical tactic will show you otherwise. You do your best firefighting on the fireground and in real life when you make a habit of thinking inside the box—as in containing the fire or the life challenge into the smallest possible box so it remains under control and you can extinguish it fully by drowning it with floods of water.

The waters you use to drown life's fires are not of the liquid variety, of course. Instead you will rely on streams of courage, self-awareness, introspection, and recaptured power. But before you get to use any of those, you have got to effectively confine the baggage holding you back from being the version of yourself you are looking to become. The key to learning Confine is mastering how well you summon the courage to move forward into your future without the baggage of your past.

Chances are you may not be that great at boxing up a hot mess of baggage and drowning it in metaphorical waters of courage and self-awareness. Do not worry—I will guide you. Most of us are not good at this, at least until we are trained to do it and we cultivate it as a skill for many years. But you do not have many years to nurture this skill; you have urgent life fires to battle right now and you need an effective solution just as urgently.

Reflection for Confine
Luckily, there is a shortcut to developing the skill to apply Confine to your baggage. It is called visioning, and it is powerful when used correctly. In a nutshell, when you use visioning to confine your baggage, what you are really doing is giving yourself a brand new frame of reference or lens through which you will see yourself from now on.

Visioning: Your New Frame of Reference
I instruct participants in my training sessions to use a simple commitment statement as the cornerstone of their visioning exercises. Something like this simple daily commitment statement is very effective when you combine it with introspection (and meditation, if you are so inclined):

- I love and forgive myself.
- I am forgiven and I am free.
- I see myself as a new and improved person, and I like what I see.

It is up to you whether you use this exact commitment statement or you tweak it to suit your own style. Whatever you decide, it is important to include the concepts of forgiveness, freedom, renewal, and self-acceptance. Often we are our own harshest critics and worst enemies in life. So much of the baggage we carry is caused by our own inability to pedal beyond our past, to forgive ourselves and free ourselves from self-imposed, unrealistic expectations and perceived shortcomings.

Confine in 3 Steps

Confine is harnessing control over experiences leading up to the current day in order to:

- change thinking
- change behavior
- create a "no drama zone"

Applying Confine means to disallow the spread or continuation of negative, unhealthy experiences into your future. At this point in the healing/growing process, we want to break free or at least begin to detach from the old baggage—to unpack, reveal, and face the truth of our lives while courageously dealing with emotions, thoughts, and behaviors that have kept us stuck. It is now time to leave the past where it belongs: in the past!

After recognizing prior troubling lifestyle habits and patterns in the previous inventory of exposure, we must build a dam of concealment around that experience and take the lessons learned, leaving behind the debilitating memories and habits. Advance successfully toward a new and improved life. In your personal and professional life, this is on the level of moving forward from the disappointment of relapses, missed goals, failed projects, bad decisions, terminations, demotions, criticism (whether constructive or destructive), and negative feedback to making these situations learning experiences that foster growth and maturity.

"Growth is an action word. This life is about forward progression to a bigger, better you!" -RKM

CPR: Save Your Own Life

While my childhood contained some traumatic, dysfunctional experiences, because I have forgiven my father for his actions I choose to learn from the experience and recall our good times together. In doing so, I can breathe and save my own life, and you can save your own life, too.

We know CPR to be cardiopulmonary resuscitation, the technique used to help save a victim from a life-threatening condition. Its purpose is to regain normal breathing and heart activity.

For me, CPR is about the care, protection, and resilience needed to overcome life challenges that threaten to break our hearts and snatch the breath of inspiration from our lungs.

CPR as it pertains to my life and my recovery of my normal breathing and emotional heart activity began when I came to understand my first hero—my father. Although I was mentally and emotionally damaged by the actions of this man, who seemed to be on a continuous search for peace, love, and stability within himself, I realized later in life that he may not have had a role model to guide him. I never met my paternal grandfather. He died before I had the opportunity to meet him. My father never spoke of him and I never had much interest in asking about him.

As a kid, I loved the ground my father walked. When he stepped out of the house on a Saturday morning, more often than not you would find Little Rodgie with him, riding "shotgun" in the passenger seat alongside him in one of his long sedans. Two of the more memorable cars were his Buick Electra 225 or his Cadillac Coupe DeVille. He would have a small cup of his favorite beverage, and I would have a grilled half smoke covered in raw onions and mustard along with a chocolate drink from a neighborhood corner store. We drove around the city to visit and hang out with one or more of his friends, or we would take the long haul to St. Mary's County, Maryland, from Southeast D.C., to visit my paternal grandmother.

Very often he would have a cup of brown liquor from the start of the drive early in the day until our return home later that evening. With the windows down and the sun shining, I enjoyed the music of The Temptations, Aretha Franklin, Joe Tex, and other soulful R&B artists as they played on the car's 8-track tape player. I was riding with my favorite guy in the world.

Success with Confine

When we succeed in the action of Confine to confine our baggage, we liberate ourselves and harness the power to leave behind that baggage for good. We achieve a heightened state of mind that is free, open to success, and able to embrace change.

There comes a time when you can no longer blame other people, places, or events, no matter how traumatic, for your current state. Therefore, you begin to take full responsibility for your stuff. A major part of moving on is to expose the old negative thinking and habits that no longer serve you as you progress healthfully toward a positive and bright future. It is time to break free, or at least begin to detach, from the old baggage—to unpack, reveal, and face the truth while courageously dealing with emotions, thoughts, and behaviors that have kept you stuck.

There is joy, health, freedom, and power in your truth. When we bravely reveal secrets that have caused stagnation, hurt, anger, and confusion in our lives, we become open to hope, happiness, and possibility.

We all have struggles in this life. Some may appear to be worse than others, such as a personal, physical, or mental challenge, or that of a child or family member. Or you might have the potential to run the fastest 50-yard dash or create the next machine that will take humanity to a place beyond our imagination, but your spirit has been spoiled, the light of hope was dimmed by a thief in your life who stole your innocence as well as your belief in yourself and in your fellow man.

In retrospect, I realize that fear and a lack of faith, mainly in self, is a hindrance to a life of growth. Now three decades later, the seed of growth has fully bloomed. It started with my first life coach and has extended to many other coaches whose training has helped to mold me into the father, husband, coach, and leader I have become. I travel near and far, delving into trainings and studies of some of the top individuals and organizations in the industry of self-development.

These dynamic development trainings spur introspective enlightenment, such as lessons on business and influence that change perspectives and create possibilities. It took decades of shedding the past while moving away from the impossible and nearer to the possible. The seed of hope, courage, and growth that lies within us all continues to bloom.

We cannot underestimate the tremendous impact of teachers, trainers, and mentors, whether formal or informal in title and function, for these are individuals assigned to your life who will guide you closer to your purpose and destiny. While humbling yourself under their tutelage and working hard to excel beyond your fears, you will learn, grow, and flourish—in that project, in learning people management—while pursuing a new business endeavor. Although the path may be dark and fiery, a work, school, or life mentor will jumpstart the process of a brand new journey.

"We talk a lot about the past, and not enough about the future. You cannot move ahead while looking back." -RKM

The Truth

When we surrender to our truth—be it good, bad, happy, or sad—we connect with our internal and external power. Too often, people run from the pain of life, hoping to find peace, power, and refuge in a lie. The truth and a lie cannot both occupy the same space. Stand in courage and grab ahold to the truth... Expose the lies!

The Ladder

Use what you gain in this phase of Confine in order to gain access to your overall success. As you ascend the ladder of success, you are enabled to turn 360 degrees around you to check all your surroundings.

The application of Confine gives you a unique perspective higher than the obstacles and fires you face. To get a breakthrough in relationships, career, health, and emotional wellbeing, you must reach for it.

Like I have mentioned earlier, this is exactly the right frame of mind from which metaphorical waters can flow. And flow they will! Get the hoses ready—it is time to extinguish.

CHAPTER 6:
EXTINGUISH

*Extinguish the fire in a flood of
strategically applied water.*

Believe it or not, you are actually at your most powerful when you are also at your most vulnerable. That is because when you are being honest with yourself, and opening yourself up completely, you let out everything; you release your vulnerabilities and unleash your true strength. That inner strength that you have been concealing along with your vulnerabilities are now free to bubble to the surface and churn the engine of change in your life. And that is exactly what you need to kickstart this life firefight into high gear.

Once we identify and confine our past baggage, the next step is to devote every resource we have in order to properly eliminate the unhealthy trappings of our past. We are literally aiming to drown our boxed up baggage like firefighters drown a fire to extinguish it.

It may surprise you to know that there is an art to applying water to drown out a fire. You do not just grab a hose and start spraying streams of water everywhere. Firefighters are trained in fire streams operations to deliver the water in the safest and most effective manner possible. It involves setting the nozzle spray pattern, preparing the hose to deliver the water, and setting the right pressure on your hose line—all before you enter the building to spray the water.

As you can see, preparing the delivery system is an important part of extinguishing the flames. Guess what? You guessed it: It is the same in real life, too. Are your water delivery systems ready? How will you apply those figurative waters of courage, self-awareness, introspection, and recaptured power that we spoke about in the last chapter?

The channels through which our waters flow in life are our minds and our hearts, sometimes quite literally. It is not by chance that a lifetime of dysfunctional living often leads to mental health issues, unbearable stress, and the heart conditions that so often accompany it. Leaving our life's fires slowly burning unchecked very often leads to mental stress and physical burnout.

When we wear ourselves out physically and emotionally, we become susceptible to stress-related conditions like what health professionals have long acknowledged as contributors or pre-cursors to even more serious conditions like heart disease, high blood pressure, and stroke—all of which if left completely unchecked can be fatal.

Reflection for Extinguish

So how do you get your water channels ready? This part of the approach is fairly easy (yes, finally something easy!) to accomplish. Getting your channels ready is part of what we have been doing all along. You are exercising mindfulness and becoming practiced in self-awareness. You are affirming your self-commitment and acceptance of yourself on a daily basis. When you do these things repeatedly and consistently, you are getting your "lines" and "water channels" prepped.

Priming the Pump

The act of releasing air from the water tank of wagon pumps is referred to as "priming the pump." When it is time to have water to extinguish a fire, nobody wants to be on the "line" to open your pipe and have to wait for water to fill the hose when fire and heat are banking down on your head.

The firefighting tactic of Extinguish allows you to dissolve your baggage, leaving the weight of yesterday behind as you move toward change. Healthy methods of change include:

- Talk it out
- Walk it out
- Cry it out
- Exercise

Success with Extinguish

Now it is time to eradicate the old and bring in the new. When enough water or other solvents dominate the fire or other dangerous source, there is no more hazard. When we replace enough with the new, fresh, and reinvented thinking and behavior, the old no longer exists. It is replaced with a newly restored system of operation.

Using all resources available, make final steps in erasing the weighted, lingering emotions, thoughts, and behaviors from yesterday's mistakes. Doing so equips you to live a life free of weighted baggage from the past. In your personal and professional life, this is on the level of a healthy after-action assessment in which you take inventory of your obstacles faced, extract what did work or can work for your success, and work it with confidence. Own it!

Is the fire out?
The biggest question I am asked about the Extinguish tactic is: When will I know when I have succeeded in extinguishing the fire? This one can be tricky to answer and even trickier to experience. The rule of thumb here is that you have successfully managed to extinguish them when:

- The fires you faced and committed to put out are no longer a constant nagging threat in your life.
- The old feelings that used to gnaw at you are quieted.
- The negative thoughts that once overpowered you and immobilized you are now kept at bay.
- The inability to make a good decision is replaced by confident decision-making.

Will it happen overnight? No, of course it will not. This makes it very different from the real life gratification of successfully extinguishing a fire. First responders at the scene of a fire know exactly when the blaze is out. Depending on the fire you are battling in your life, you may not be able to precisely pinpoint the moment you have put out the fire after months of working through Rescue, Expose, and Confine.

Sometimes it can seem as though nothing is posing an immediate danger from the outside but on the inside, the fires rage. That was the case for me. I recall my younger self standing in the driveway of my semi-detached home in Northeast D.C., on the phone with a friend, feeling hopeless, helpless, and suicidal. There I was in my early 30s—a father, son, brother, friend, and public servant. I owned a car and had a closet full of clothes and stylish shoes. The refrigerator I enjoyed. I had everything to live for and feel grateful for, but what is on the outside is not always an indication of the real truth on the inside.

For the majority of my life, I had been uncomfortable with myself, unhappy with who I was, and disconnected from my real purpose and my gift to share with the world. Quite frankly, I felt like the opposite of a gift—an unhappy, lost, angry, and unworthy burden. In my attempt to find my place in the world and experience the happiness I saw the people in television sitcoms, commercials, and billboards portray, I further lost touch with the happy little fellow born in New Haven, Connecticut, and raised in the Chocolate City of real life.

I can remember as early as elementary school having my first taste of beer. For the next 27 years, I would use alcohol and other mind-altering substances to help me fill the void of self-worth and spiritual connection that I would later find following my decision to surrender, give myself a chance at a new way of living, and win. I was a guy who felt everything but capable, able, and grateful. It was my mentality of victimization that kept me stuck in a rut of entitlement to emotional suffering and complaint. I wanted to give up on life because I felt dying was easier than living life.

Despite my blessings, my level of selfishness gave me the right to only think of me and how I felt as I ignored the feelings and rights of my loved ones who loved me, cared for me, and depended on me—namely my daughters, who needed my love, attention, guidance, and protection. My mother and father also wanted their adult son to continue to grow into a man of success in every aspect of life.

It was a long road toward overcoming fears of the future, failure, and a lack of faith before I started on the road of recovery and self-discovery. I continue to practice a life of faith, trust, and courage. I understand that the grace of a universal God has saved me from a life of anguish, pain, and possibly an early death.

As I have remained free of alcohol with a sober mind and lifted spirit, I have an awareness and acceptance of grace that has restored me to a life of love for self and others. It is my daily prayer that I learn to submit my will to the will of God, the spirit of love and orderly direction that dwells within us all. This sense of hope, faith, and courage to persevere is what I have been searching for all along, the feeling that everything will be OK.

Rebuilding Your Life

To rebuild your life is to become aware of who you are and what you are. The purpose of extinguishment is to get rid of old thinking and behaviors. Drown them with new and improved thoughts, feelings, skills, and plans. Set goals for the purpose of helping you to focus and thrive toward a meaningful target. Make it your aim to totally smother the destructive fire of your past with streams of powerful and purposeful visions of a future packed with energy, passion, and a commitment to growth.

At the age of 29, I was hired as a D.C. firefighter. I had just made it under the cutoff age of 30 at that time. Thankfully in my early 20s, I had responded to the constant nudge (both verbal and physical) of the man who would become my Taekwondo instructor, Mr. Neal. I came to Taekwondo not knowing much about it and not having a specific goal at the start. This Korean style of self-defense opened me up to a world of mental, emotional, and physical fitness I had no idea I possessed. Mr. Neal was a man of tremendous physical strength, emotional balance, and awareness of character and talent.

During my active 20-year commitment to the tenets of Taekwondo, Mr. Neal invested in me time, attention, and concern that are normally displayed by a father to his children. Mr. Neal's hard training drills and a medical ability to partner individuals for the purpose of personal growth within each person was masterful. I felt courageous and assured in front of one classmate opponent while feeling less assured in front of another. However, I felt safe and ready to learn when in front of a notably more experienced and technically skilled opponent. Taekwondo tested me in every area of my life—my fears, ego, tenacity, commitment, and desire.

Taekwondo had been a part of my life for 10 years prior to my quitting alcohol. I do not want to imagine my physical condition had I not been practicing the discipline of physical fitness and pushing myself beyond my normal limits. I am thankful for my practice and study of Taekwondo as an investment that continues to pay off.

Upon earning my green belt of ascension toward black belt, I had taken a few knocks against almost every part of my body, had dished out a few, grew in confidence, skill, knowledge, and delight, and was ready for more. With his practice of old school "knuckles down" pushups and mental gymnastics, Mr. Neal prepared me for life and everything that comes with it.

His brother Clarence Neal, who happens to be married to my sister Tasha, was there for me in my late teens, when I was fresh out of love and about to be a father. He was my informal, unpaid "life coach" before it became a popular position. "Neal," as we affectionately refer to him, walked me through my feelings, duties, and expectations—those expected of me and what I could expect from others. About 98 percent of the time, he was spot on!

I was young and filled with potential but I had no idea of how to tap into it. Neal would sit and talk to me about life. I was still very uncertain about being a father and did not have much to offer in the way of emotional support or knowledge of how to care for a baby girl. That is where my sister Tasha came in. She threw out the net of love that surrounded her three children and the children of my brother and two other sisters. Her home was always filled with food, fun, love, and support. I especially needed her and my brother-in-law at that time, and I thank God that they were there.

Neal told me how my life would go after becoming a young father crushed from my first heartbreak. He gave me pointers on how to approach people and situations in order to safely navigate and get through. As he talked, my eyes were open but my mind was closed. I would come back to him with the same scenarios again and again, and as a result I would have the same experiences with the same lessons to learn. After a while, he dubbed me a "slow bloomer." I did not act on his proven method of success for my life until the pain of doing it my way became too much to bear. Things he spoke of months earlier took months for me to accept and try.

The past can affect your present.
It was almost 35 years before I could be in a household environment, hear a sudden loud noise, and not experience a jolt in my mind and emotions that took me

back to my childhood home where an act of anger had been carried out through violent, physical force. This, through a child's eyes, is one of the most painful and terrifying experiences in life—to see the two people you love the most trample and be trampled upon. Emotionally, I was empty and unbalanced.

On I went, growing and aching while slowly shedding the pains and thoughts of confusion from my past. I had another biological daughter as I helped to raise and love her sister as my own. Single with three girls watching my every move as a man and their father, I continued falling, getting up, and moving forward. I had spent over 20 years using alcohol to run away from pain of the past, thereby making it difficult to get to know and love me or anyone else because I continued to run away from myself instead of toward myself.

The Burning Room: Trust, Training, Courage, Service
A clearly visible fire can be a "cake walk" for a firefighter opposed to the steadily growing flames that cannot be seen but only felt! I had to cautiously and aggressively push my way through the darkness of heavy black smoke toward the base of a fire that continuously grew in size and temperature. While this was a part of my professional life, it was the reality for my personal life beforehand. It also applies to anyone who wants to smother the hotspots within before they grow into hellfire that can destroy lives.

There is a particular emergency call that still stands out in my mind. The "box alarm" for a house rang out at approximately nine o'clock one morning. We pulled into the block and saw dark smoke pushing from under the eaves of a single family home. Fully geared up, I jumped off the piece, grabbed my 200 feet of hose, and entered the front door of the house. I made my way through the ground floor, advancing my hose to the second level. The smoke was thick and black. There were obstructions in the tight hallway of the second floor as I began to feel the heat but there was little sign of fire. It was nearly impossible to see one foot in front of me. The environment was stacked with the dangers of carcinogens, household chemicals, unseen obstacles, and the threat of hidden fire. This is the time when a firefighter has to rely on trust and training. I trusted my senses and relied on my experience as I made my way toward the flames of hell.

After searching the nearest bedroom, I felt the rise in temperature and continued on one knee back into the common area of the second floor into an adjoining bedroom where I met the raging flames. This was actually a brief moment of relief to have found the source of danger and destruction. I opened the pipe and held the line as the highly pressured water began to drown the flames, which had engulfed every inch of the room.

To have safely completed the assignment of saving life and property is one of the most rewarding feelings that a firefighter experiences. Some say it is a noble and courageous act of duty. I have found it to be an honor and a privilege to serve and protect the residents of and visitors to our nation's capital.

The Truth

What you have to accept when battling fires in your life is that the ability to extinguish them is really a journey you will take. It is a little more of a tactical destination than a tactical action, and you get to decide when you have arrived at that destination and strategically sprayed all of your metaphorical water. When you feel that you are ready to move ahead to the final tactic, Overhaul, you are one small step from completing my RECEO firefighting program. So get fired up—you are almost done!

CHAPTER 7: OVERHAUL

*Overhaul is a never-ending quest
for a fire-free life.*

Before we launch into my final tactic, it is worth reflecting on the chapter title for a moment. Overhaul is never-ending, as in it goes on forever. Now that you have gotten your mindset ready for the Overhaul tactic, let us jump in.

In the firefighting business, the Overhaul tactic is finite, and it is one of the most important steps. It is also a tactic that is probably familiar to most people outside the business. Overhaul is when firefighters take a final look at a fire scene, searching for hotspots or hidden fires lurking in the rubble needing to be put out.

Reflection for Overhaul

When fighting life fires, Overhaul follows Extinguish (remember, it is a conscious decision to achieve extinguishment). Overhaul is a long-term commitment that you choose to make and that you map out carefully to ensure the best possible chance of your continued success. Think of it as a maintenance plan.

In Overhaul, you develop and put into motion a plan of continuous action toward your evolving, better self and your desired goals. The objective of Overhaul is to breathe differently, think differently, and behave differently. You can overhaul—or change the direction of your scope—by:

- taking a step back
- gaining a different perspective
- setting goals
- planning
- focusing

When you have a plan or a tactical strategy to follow to stay successful, you are far more likely to actually sustain your fire-free life. Your plan must include strategies for maintaining your new mindset, effectively and swiftly addressing any issues as they present themselves (as well as being proactive before they become setbacks), and employing an ongoing method for self-reflection and personal renewal.

Your tactics do not need to be lengthy to be effective. A daily morning commitment statement takes two minutes. Time for mindful thinking and self-reflection can mean taking 10 minutes of time for yourself carved out at lunch time or before bed. I suggest investing in motivational reading materials that reflect your personal interests.

Success with Overhaul

Let us say that you are a golfer. Part of your Overhaul plan might include studying methods to improve your golf game. *How does this help*, you might ask? You are expanding your capacity to get better at doing something you enjoy. You are opening your mind to learning and accepting new concepts. This keeps your mind open and receptive to other things as well.

If you are a food lover or a cook, explore new cooking techniques and experiment with new recipes. Go outside your comfort zone. Try your hand at preparing food you enjoy from other cultures. Master a new dish and add it to your routine.

As you expand your horizons during the Overhaul phase, do not forget to invite other people to share in your newfound or newly honed skills. Make a habit of inviting supportive, positive-thinking family and friends to surround you. It is very important to keep company with those who are positive and who will boost you ahead on your journey. Having a support system or network of allies surrounding you will help ensure long-term success.

I want to emphasize the importance of choosing the right people to surround you. As hard as it may be to separate yourself from negative thinkers and naysayers, especially if you have spent much of your lifetime trapped in relationships with negative people, you must make the decision to change your people surroundings to reflect your new life outlook. If you do not, you seriously increase your chances for long-term failure.

Imagine that you have been on a diet to change your lifestyle and you have reached your goal weight. Your maintenance plan would never include stocking your pantry and fridge with cakes, cookies, and pies! Think of your Overhaul plan the same way. It is meant to ensure your long-term success and health, and you must craft it thoughtfully and commit to executing it to the best of your ability, to live your fire-free life.

This really happened, and I am glad.
I am going to take you back to my young self, the one who embarked on a journey of spending 20 years choosing not to commit to a woman in a relationship because of initial heartbreak I had experienced. It came from issues in my upbringing, fear, immaturity, and choosing first of all not to commit to myself. But one day, I took a chance. After being a father of two biological girls and one I loved and cared for just like my own, in late December 2001 I was not in any committed relationship. I began to see an old acquaintance from our teen years who I had known for more than 25 years. Dana was a pretty, innocent 13-year-old church girl, and I was 16 years old, on the cusp of jumping into a world of parties, fantasies, and only God knows what else. I would tease her that she had a crush on me, when it was clearly the other way around!

We were connected through our mutual niece, Tamicka. In their early 20s, my brother and her sister married and had a daughter. Although their marriage ended in divorce, we both stayed connected to the child of their union. I always felt a strong desire and need to spend time with our mutual niece, and we would maintain a close relationship.

Dana and I both grew into adulthood, navigating our way through the many challenges of life in the big city. Our lives took two different paths. Over the next two decades, she would begin a steady career, marry, have a daughter, and come full circle back to her mother's. My next two decades were a bit more colorful. After my biggest regret of dropping out of high school in 1979 and four years later obtaining my GED, I worked several jobs, from roofer to janitor, construction worker, short order cook, duct worker, bindery operator, car salesman, and firefighter. Mine was not one of a single career path, but it cannot be said that I was not on the hunt!

During my visits to pick up my niece from her grandmother's house, I would ask about her aunt Dana. I learned that her relationship status had changed; mine had also changed and the stars were aligning. After several denied proposals for a date, a "yes" finally rose from beneath the many layers of "no's."

After more than 25 years ago and four children later, we had our first date. We have been married since 2004 with a happy blended family that includes an additional child. What was once "I" is now "we" ... and we are happy!

Set a New Course
It is now time to set your life on a new course of direction and action. We have faced the horrors of our distant and recent past—the past that held us back, made us feel

ashamed, uncertain, and stuck. As a result of actively facing "the man/woman in the mirror," this is an opportunity to build on the accomplishments born out of the work in earlier experiences of introspection and rebuilding, which created a renewed sense of personal value and self-worth.

Let us overcome what we once thought was insurmountable and build a life we can be proud of—a life of victories and triumphs. Revamp the resume! Add valuable training, education, experience that you have taken for granted. Approach the project that you are stuck in from a different perspective. Try something new in the relationship with yourself and others.

As I mentioned several chapters back, you do not need to undertake the tactical steps of RECEO in precise order for them to be effective. For firefighters facing a burning building, knowing which steps to use and when becomes instinctive once you have faced enough fires.

As you battle your life's fires, you can also rely on your instincts to guide you to the right place to start the order in which to undertake the steps. It could be that instead of starting with the Rescue tactic, you start with the Confine tactic and move backward to Expose and Rescue. Or maybe you find it is easier to begin with Expose and move to Confine and then on to Extinguish before you feel that you reached the point of Rescue.

Keep this book handy to review the lessons you have learned in it, to refer to information about how to execute the steps for yourself, and for affirmation that you are on the right track. Do not be discouraged. Do not give up. Do not succumb to the fires! When you fall short of your goals, do not take the setback as a failure. Instead, get right back up and get back on track. Winners never quit and quitters never win. Here is another good, hardworking cliché that is never wrong.

You have probably also heard that anything worth doing is worth doing right. And that if something great was easy, then everyone would be doing it. Yes, these are also cliché, but as I told you when we got started on this journey together, nuggets of truth can often be found in even the most overworked expressions, and these little gems fall into that category. Take RECEO and master it to build a better life for yourself. And even if you fall short, you have still come one step closer to winning because the firefighting tactics are becoming familiar to you and easier to execute. And the next time you try, you will be prepared for what to avoid or overcome on the road to success.

For each one of us, the journey to a fire-free life is different and so too are our roadmaps for victory. Know that the goal is not to spend a lifetime beating back the flames of discord and turbulence in your life. Use what you have learned from my life-adapted RECEO tactics to chart a course for your ultimate success battling the firestorms in your own life, reacting when you have to— but more frequently relying on proactive, mindful thinking—to keep the fires from flaring up again in the wonderful life you create for yourself.

The intent of me writing my story for you is to make the connection that we all share as people, in families facing struggles that create pain and anger, frustration, and sometimes mental and physical anguish. Through my struggle—our struggle—we learn to look within and around us for the strength, guidance, and love that carries us through each day, one day at a time. I mentioned earlier that we discover the power of love through sharing and connecting with others of similar trials, and sometimes connecting with those of unlikely similarities.

What I continue to learn most, as I sit on the other side of those struggles and necessary lessons, is that "I matter." I stood up for my mother, "a love of my life," and now I need to stand up for myself—stand up for the little boy whose spirit was broken, who wanted to fly but did not feel like he had the wings or the energy to get off the ground—stand up for the child who watched helplessly and painfully with tears of fear rushing down his brown face. Stand up for the new feeling of love for self and the new understanding of each individual being responsible for their personal behavior. I was not responsible for the actions of anyone outside of that little brown-skinned, red-haired, big-eared boy they called "Rodgie." As for me, life has been a journey of lessons and blessings.

The Truth

The human being is a resilient creature. Throughout so many stories of pain, suffering, trauma, and emotional turmoil, we still fight back—we fight to get to that place of peace and sanity somewhere within the center of our being. We all do not make it to our center at the same time or pace. Some settle for staying in the same emotional and mental rut, year after year, decade after decade, sometimes generation after generation. I guess that is part of the reason there continues to be so much turmoil in the world; a planet of people with different experiences, at different locations, and different perspectives, all wanting to get from the place of pain and discourse to a place of happiness. I would like to think that we are all aiming for happiness within ourselves as individuals, and for happiness with the world around us.

I would also like to think that as we live and share this space of existence with family, friends, and strangers, we will continue to learn from, accept, forgive, and be forgiven for life's mistakes. I have come to the conclusion that outside of skin color, cultural beliefs, and rituals, we are all the same. When I am able to accept myself for who I am inside and out, I will be able to accept you as well. As I see it, the ultimate desire for every human being on earth is to be happy. The road we each take to get there can be tricky.

Choose to take responsibility for the creation of a life you can be happy with—a life that feeds your soul as it emanates from the core of your being. Build a life that is an example for others to follow. Work on yourself so that you can be a vessel of hope and inspiration to others.

These principles of action have all been proven effective in the fire industry for decades. In their modified form, I encourage you to accept them and apply them to your life. You will raise the temperature of your success!

In all that you do, be sure to:

FINISH STRONG, FINISH STRONG, AND FINISH STRONG!

SOME HELPFUL TOOLS

I have modified these concepts, life-saving techniques, and actions to apply to individuals and/or groups for the purpose of offering practical tools of motivation, mental enlightenment, and a sense of direction toward a path of future success.

"All clear" — a phrase used on the emergency ground to signal hazards that have been reduced, and it is a safe place to operate within. After the work of RECEO has been tested and put into action, the hazard of negative thoughts, emotions, and actions have been exposed and dealt with. Opportunity for forgiveness, self-awareness, and growth awaits. Despite the images and messages of fear and despair, the world is a safe place. Immerse yourself with thoughts of beauty, love, and power. Use your power of choice.

SOGs — Standard operating guidelines are an established set of rules and policies maintained for effective operation of Fire Department activity. What are your core values, beliefs, standards, and expectations? How do you operate within the dynamics of family, business, and personal activities? As you progress in each of these areas of your life, it is imperative to operate from your established set of SOGs. A mentor can help you map them all out while holding you accountable to these intangible floorplans for living through emergencies.

PPV — Positive pressure ventilation is a method of clearing a structure of toxic, hazardous air by pulling in clean, outside air to forcibly replace the heavy air of carcinogens and other toxicities. How do you clear the air of hazards? In real life this is achieved by adding positive people, positive thoughts, and positive actions to your life that heavily outweigh the negative pull of doubt, fear, and uncertainty. If your current environment does not support your freedom to express, create, and breathe, then maybe the use of PPV could be an effective tool of action.

Rescue — On the scene of a fire emergency, the firefighter's number one priority is to provide a means of egress for any possible trapped firefighter or persons. This same concept can also be used to bring attention to the individual or group by making them aware of the part they can play in the rescue, redevelopment, and enhancement of their lives.

Expose — This element is used to help the client recognize the behaviors and thoughts from their past that continue a negative pattern in the present. Self-examination, introspection, and honesty are key factors at this level.

Confine — After recognizing prior, troubling lifestyle habits and patterns in the previous inventory of exposure, it is encouraged that the client/clients build a dam of concealment around that experience and take the lessons learned, leaving behind the debilitating memories and habits, while moving toward a new and improved life.

Extinguish — Using all resources available, make final steps in erasing the weighted, lingering emotions, thoughts, and behaviors from yesterday's mistakes. You are prepared to live a life free of baggage from the past.

Overhaul — As a result of actively facing "the man in the mirror," this is an opportunity to build upon the accomplishments born out of the work in earlier experiences of inner cleansing and rebuilding, which created a sense of renewed self-worth and freedom from the past. Dream big. Set goals. Create strategies. Keep moving and never stop! Go forward with purpose, passion, and zeal!

Teamwork — Working as a team and developing leadership skills are essential. "Two in, two out" as a rule; have someone to bounce and share ideas with. Go for it together and benefit from the beginnings of teamwork. In my profession, we say "follow the line" because your team is your lifeline. Remain in touch with your line. Everyone has a different and vital role to play with the greater purpose of connecting in order to extend the line and get the job done with excellence. This involves:

- Making the proper connections through networking to extend the lines of your dreams

- Supporting others through the concept of the "eat together, fight together" rule that means when your back is against the wall and your life is on the line, it is important and comforting to know you have someone on your side who you have bonded with—from the training room to the dining hall to the emergency room

- Working together through the "two in, two out" rule relating to teamwork and family; the "we go in together, we stay together, we come out together" mindset begins the minute a team begins to form at the outset of basic firefighter training and also applies to your career and/or family team in order to build trust and reliance on each other

Team members should know their predetermined positions based on the order in which they were called and the proximity of the emergency to an individual house—or the job at hand in their professional and personal lives.

It is my desire to have the challenges I have faced and grown through be a testament and example of how to go through, what to do, and maybe what not to do.

The internal fire can be used to produce or destroy.
Redirect your fire of anger and pain into love and joy.

Learn to use your burning desire
for the development of yourself and others.
Be brave, be committed, be teachable—unleash your inner
firefighter for self-love and to serve another.

About the Author

Born in New Haven, Connecticut, and raised in Washington, D.C., Roderick K. Mitchell is a husband and father to five beautiful girls. After successfully celebrating 28 years in a meaningful career of public service as a firefighter with the Washington, D.C. Fire/EMS Department, he commits full time to his passion of training, writing, and being an active keynote speaker that empowers audiences nationwide. A broad range of organizations and businesses have benefited from his informative, inspiring, and engaging presentations. Mitchell's love for the community is displayed through his volunteer work in area schools, non-profits, and adult detention centers. His first book, *Fire, Fury, Faith: A Story of Success by Fire*, is a culmination of lessons learned for optimal success to benefit young adults, professionals, and anyone looking to improve life's outlook.

For booking inquiries, please email Mr. Roderick K. Mitchell: roderick@successbyfire.com